D0490133

DISCARDED

KUPER ACADEMY LIBRARY

2 4 4 a

Kuper Academy
2 Aesop
Kirkland, Qc
H9H 5G5

J574.5264
STO ✓

MOUNTAINS

Lynn M. Stone

ROURKE ENTERPRISES, INC.
Vero Beach, FL 32964

Photo Credits:

© Jerry Hennen 8, 32; © Tom and Pat Leeson 1, 31, 37; © Lynn M. Stone cover, cover inset, 5, 9, 11, 14, 15, 19, 23, 25, 27, 33, 35, 38, 41, 45.

© 1989 Rourke Enterprises, Inc.

All rights reserved. No part of this book may be reproduced or utilized in any form or by any means, electronic or mechanical including photocopying, recording or by any information storage and retrieval system without permission in writing from the publisher.

Library of Congress Cataloging in Publication Data

Stone, Lynn M.
   Mountains / by Lynn M. Stone.
      p. cm. — (Ecozones)
   Includes index.
   Summary: Examines the mountainous community as an ecological niche and describes the plant and animal life supported there.
   ISBN 0-86592-448-1
   1. Mountain ecology—Juvenile literature.   2. Mountains—Juvenile literature. [1. Mountain ecology. 2. Ecology.] I. Title.
II. Series: Stone, Lynn M.   Ecozones.
QH541.5.M65S76   1989
574.5'264—dc20   89-32747
                                                        CIP
                                                         AC

CONTENTS

MOUNTAINS

The sweeping view from the top of a mountain is remarkably different from the confined view below. Life on a mountaintop is also different.

In Arizona or Colorado you can stand in mountain foothills covered by grass. Above you, on a mountaintop not far away, will be Arctic plants growing in a cold Arctic climate.

The changes in mountain life, from bottom to top, don't occur instantly at one spot on the mountain, nor does the grand view from a mountain's top appear immediately. As a hiker climbs, the view beyond the mountain begins to emerge and the plants and animals on the mountain change. Not only because of the views, but also because of the many different plant and animal communities, mountains are one of the most appealing places in nature. There is no better place than a mountain for seeing a variety of living things from many **life zones** in a compact area.

At times, it's hard to tell whether the hill that looms ahead is really a mountain. In the broadest sense of the word, a mountain can be any large,

Opposite *Rugged Rocky Mountains offer spectacular views of rock summits, lakes, and wildlife.*

uplifted mass of ground that stands apart from the land around it. No agreed upon minimums for height or shape have been established for mountains. The most impressive mountains, of course, are those that rise abruptly from their surroundings.

Whether or not the landform is a mountain often depends on local interpretation. Everyone can agree that the 14,000-foot peaks of the Rocky Mountains are truly mountains. But where less commanding landforms are present, their designation as "mountain," "highland," "ridge," or "hill" is often a matter of choice—and some disagreement.

The ancient Hanging Hills of Meriden, Connecticut, are uplifts of ancient volcanic activity. One of the hills is Mount Higby. It stands 892 feet above the terrain below. In the mountainous American West, Mount Higby would more accurately be called a ridge or hill.

The assigners of the name "Mount Higby" may have exaggerated slightly, but consider Mount Dora, Florida. The highest point of land anywhere in Florida is 345 feet above sea level, and it's not in the town of Mount Dora. In contrast, an 8,500-foot peak of ice and rock on Baffin Island, Canada, is called Penny Highland.

The high country generally considered mountains in North America varies from the comparatively low, worn Appalachians in the East to the mighty, snow-capped peaks of the Rockies, Cascades, Sierra Nevadas, and Coast Ranges in the West. The central interior of the continent is generally flat or rolling between the Appalachians and the Rockies. Even though the land actually slopes upward, it does so quite gradually and usually without the obvious uplifting of ground we describe as mountainous. In western Canada, the great ranges of mountains are almost inseparable as they arc into Alaska, which is ridged with several chains of mountains.

East of Alaska and across the "top" of North America, many of Canada's Arctic islands are lumped with snowy, barren rock mountains. The coasts of Greenland in northeastern North America are also quite mountainous.

A cluster of low mountains and hills—the Wichitas of southwest Oklahoma, the Ouachitas of Arkansas and Oklahoma, and the Ozarks of Missouri and Arkansas—is the only extensive complex of highlands between the Rockies and Appalachians. The Black Hills of South Dakota lie somewhat east of the Wyoming Rockies, but they are a

Above *Dawn lights the snow cap of Mt. Rainier in Washington Cascades.*

part of the Rockies uplift.

Here and there in the West are comparatively small, isolated mountains. The Blue-Wallowa Mountains of northeast Oregon, for example, are islands of high ground in essentially flat country.

One of the interesting features of North American mountains is their effect on climate. As everyone who has climbed a mountain knows, the summit is cooler than the base. That seems odd because the top of a mountain is closer to the sun than the bottom, and heat rises. The air, however, becomes thinner at upper elevations. Thin air absorbs less radiant heat from the sun. Consequently the temperature drops three degrees Fahrenheit for every 1,000 feet of elevation.

Another climatic effect of mountains is their ability to wring moisture from clouds. Winds forced upward by mountain barriers cool the mountain air. Moisture condenses in the cooled air and falls as rain or snow on the mountains. By forcing prevailing winds to rise, mountains often gather a mountain lion's share of precipitation. This is particularly true on the west side of the Pacific Coast Ranges.

TYPES OF MOUNTAINS

Mountains vary tremendously in extent and character. Their roots in **geologic** events differ, and the comparative **biological** richness of mountains differs. Certainly their appearance varies. They may be gentle, green lumps or thickets of rock spires thrusting into the sky. They may be the dens of **glaciers**, gigantic frozen rivers of ice. Most mountains are robed with trees, but their caps may be snow, rock, wild garden, or trees.

The Appalachians, the major range in the East, begin in Newfoundland and stretch southwest into Georgia and northeastern Alabama. The tallest peak in these ancient mountains is Mount Mitchell at 6,684 feet above sea level in North Carolina. By comparison, Mount McKinley in the Alaska Range is the continent's highest peak at 20,320 feet, and several peaks in the Rockies exceed 14,000 feet. But the Appalachians are not without deep valleys, rushing streams, and splendidly rugged terrain.

Like other major ranges, the Appalachians are composed of closely related chains of mountains. Each of

Opposite *Southern Appalachians, often wreathed in mist, nurture lush hardwood forests.*

these chains or clusters within the whole of the Appalachian complex has its own identity. One of the notable chains is the White Mountain group in New Hampshire and its Presidential Range.

Mount Washington, at 6,290 feet, is the highest point in the United States east of the Black Hills and north of the Great Smoky Mountains. Its greater fame lies in the fact that its rocky and often snow-lit summit rises 4,500 feet directly from the surrounding lowlands. Mount Washington also enjoys some notoriety. The highest recorded wind-speed anywhere—231 miles per hour— was clocked on its bare summit in 1934.

MOUNTAINS

The storied Adirondacks of New York, many of them jutting from the huge Adirondack State Park, are neighbors of the Northern Appalachians of New England. The New England mountains and the Adirondacks share similar features: boulder-littered slopes, rich forests of mixed needle-leaved and broad-leaved trees, and the presence of many streams and lakes.

One of the characteristics that separates mountain ranges is their history. Although the Adirondacks and Northern Appalachians swell up from nearby ground, each has a separate geologic history. The Adirondacks are an extension into the United States of a tremendous, extremely old rock shield that mantles a large part of Canada.

In the Southern Appalachians, the mountains known as the Great Smokies are legendary. Like many of the Southern mountains, the Smokies are often cloaked in mist and fog. This moisture has helped produce in these mountains the richest hardwood forests in North America. In the Smokies and elsewhere throughout the Southern Appalachians, lush forests, racing waters, and spectacular blooms of spring shrubs and flowers are characteristic.

Above *Mt. McKinley, highest peak in North America, looms 20,320 feet above sea level in Alaska Range.*

The Western mountain ranges are to many people the most impressive landforms on the continent. The mightiest of these ranges is the Rockies. From the snowy, 5,000-foot peaks of the Brooks Range in Alaska, south through Canada and the United States into Mexico, the Rockies form part of the largest mountain chain on earth. They eventually become the Andes of South America.

The Rockies have hundreds of peaks that tower between 10,000 and 14,000 feet with crowns of snow and barren rock above timber line. In the

Canadian Rockies especially, glaciers are plentiful. Several of the most impressive sections of the Rockies are set aside in a chain of national parks— Rocky Mountain in Colorado, Grand Teton in Wyoming, Yellowstone in Wyoming and Montana, Glacier in Montana, and Glacier, Yoho, Waterton Lakes, Jasper, and Banff in Canada. All of the parks offer spectacular views, hiking, climbing, and a haven for mountain plants and animals.

The Sierra Nevada is a nearly solid wall of tall mountains along California's eastern boundary. It is not interrupted

Above *Glaciers, frozen rivers of ice and snow, are plentiful in the cradles of the Canadian Rockies.*

by the gaps that punctuate the Rockies.

Some of the granite rock outcroppings of the Sierras are distinctly dome-shaped. Another feature of the Sierras is the prominence of water. Proportionately, the Sierra Nevada has more water basins than any of the mountain ranges in the mainland United States. Yosemite National Park in the Sierras has 425 lakes along with abundant streams and Yosemite Falls, with a 2,430-foot plunge, the highest waterfall in North America.

The west side of the Coast Ranges, which gird the Pacific coast from northern California to British Columbia, is moist and heavily forested. In the northern section of the Coast Ranges, on the Olympic Peninsula of Washington, are the valley rain forests, the wettest land sites in the continental United States. The best known peak is Mount Olympus, rising 7,965 feet above the Pacific.

The Cascades Range stretches north from northern California into Oregon, Washington, and southern British Columbia. The Cascades are higher than the Coast Ranges with seven peaks over 10,000 feet. The champion among them is Mount Rainier at 14,408 feet. Volcanic activity, typical of the Cascades, reduced Rainier from a 16,000-

foot mountain to its present size long ago. More recent volcanic eruptions in the Cascades have rocked Lassen Peak (1921), Mount Baker (1870), and Mount St. Helens (1980).

Snow-clad and rocky, Mount Rainier is a spectacular sight as it rises 8,000 feet above the forests and mountain meadows at its feet. No less than 26 glaciers guard Rainier's flanks.

Other jewels in the Cascades are Mount Shasta and Lassen Peak in California, Mount Baker in Washington, and Mount Hood and Mount Mazama in Oregon. Mazama, at 7,000 feet, is not particularly impressive as Western Mountains go, but the cone of this ancient volcano is six-mile-wide Crater Lake. The strikingly blue water of the 2,000-foot deep lake, protected in Crater Lake National Park, has long been a source of wonder.

Above *A mountain brook bubbles through Vermont's Green Mountains. Streams delight hikers in mountains east and west.*

17

3 | MAKING OF THE MOUNTAINS

Majestic, snow-capped mountain ranges suggest that mountains are not only grand, but permanent as well. They seem too sturdy and imposing to be changed by the elements. Yet we need recall no further back than 1980. The volcano inside Washington State's Mount St. Helens exploded and tore away some 1,400 feet of the mountain's top.

Mountains are not nearly as stable and permanent as we may think. It is true that all of them are very, very old by our standards of time. The Rockies may have taken 10 million years to rise. In comparison to the Appalachians, the Rockies are youthful, at least in geologic time, which attempts to measure the earth's lengthy history. The Appalachians have generally round contours, the result of weathering by wind and rain. The Rockies are tall and sharp-crested. They have not endured the millions of years of exposure that have worn the Appalachians. Some rocks from Appalachian mountains are, scientists believe, over one billion years old. Nevertheless, mountain ranges weather

Opposite Glaciers have played an important role in shaping mountains and influencing their vegetation.

away over long periods of time. Some, like Mount St. Helens, virtually fall overnight.

The formation of the mountains unquestionably involved disturbances of great magnitude deep within the earth. But to explain the precise origins of these geologic events and the precise times at which they occurred is impossible. Scientists, however, have advanced several theories about the formation of mountains.

One of the most recent involves plate tectonics. This theory suggests that the outermost portion of the earth—the continents and oceans—are situated on plates. Heat generated from deep within the earth causes the plates to move. Mountains, according to the theory, rise mostly along the plate boundaries. Their formation seems to be caused by the collision of the plates and the stirring of volcanic forces under the earth's crust.

Mysteries abound in attempting to explain the formation of mountains. What seems to be clear is that mountain-building—and breaking down—is an ongoing process. Mountains are continually being shaped and worn by the sandblasting of wind and the effects of water. Water seeps between rocks, freezes, and expands, cracking and splintering rocks. On a grander scale, glaciers gouge and claw the very mountains they snuggle against. Streams eat their way through mountains, creating valleys and dumping sediments from the heights somewhere below.

4

PLANTS
OF THE MOUNTAINS

Whatever their elevation, location, or geologic history, mountains concentrate a variety of natural communities. From the base of a mountain to the uppermost alpine zone, the land above the trees, are apt to be several communities. Associated plants, and to a lesser extent associated animals, are arranged somewhat like belts around a mountain. This arrangement of different communities, changing as one ascends a mountain, is called **zonation**.

Each plant zone has within it characteristic species. Some of these plants overlap to the zone above or below, but generally each zone is distinct from the others. Most North American mountains south of the Arctic are clothed in trees, and the types of trees that are present determine the various life zones.

Zonation is basically the product of temperature, and temperature is affected by **latitude**. The average temperature of Chicago, for example, is cooler than the average temperature of Louisville, because Chicago is farther north. Temperature, however, is also influenced by altitude. Recall that for each

Opposite Catawba *rhododendron herald the arrival of summer in the misty Southern Appalachians of North Carolina.*

1,000 feet traveled upward, there is a corresponding loss of three degrees Fahrenheit.

The types of forests on a mountain, then, are largely the consequence of increasingly cold air. Other environmental factors that affect the development of mountain forests are soil, precipitation, wind, and exposure. Different plants have varying tolerances for the conditions in which they can live. As environmental conditions change with altitude, soil, sunlight, and other factors, the plants change accordingly. They grow where the conditions are best—or at least marginal—for their survival. When the tolerance threshold of one species has been reached, another takes its place. As one travels up the mountain path, the plants along the way change in response to the changing conditions.

The Western mountain forests are composed largely of conifers. Coniferous trees bear their seeds in cones. They are generally needle-leaved and remain green throughout the year. Spruces, firs, and pines are typical conifers. The Eastern mountain forests, except at high altitudes, are made up largely of broad-leaved trees. These trees are deciduous, which means they enter a **dormant** stage by shedding their leaves each fall.

The plant zonation of one mountain is not identical to the zonation of another. Too many environmental factors affect each location for any two peaks to be alike. Generally, however, a mountain climber in a northern latitude would reach timberline sooner than a climber in a more southern latitude.

The most distinctive mountain life zones are the **alpine** communities. One of the alpine communities is the alpine tundra. This community develops only at altitudes above which trees can no

Below *Alpine meadows of Mt. Rainier National Park spring into carpets of colorful blooms each August.*

longer grow. Few peaks in the East extend above the timber. Those that do are Mount Marcy and Mount McIntyre in the Adirondacks, Mount Katahdin in Maine, and a handful of peaks in the Presidential Range of New Hampshire.

Mountain trees begin to vanish when conditions become Arctic-like. Extreme cold, high winds, and poor soil inevitably conspire to limit the growth of forest. The last of the trees in the high mountains, their upward reach pruned by the wind's bite, often spread in twisted, mat-like thickets called *krummholz*. Above the krummholz, on mountain summits, the ground may be colonized by grasses, **sedges**, and **herbs** in a carpet of vegetation known as alpine tundra.

Alpine tundra is similar to the vegetation of the vast plains ringing the Arctic. There are no caribou, lemmings, or snow geese here, but the treelessness, the harsh climate, and the **lichen**-spotted rocks all suggest the true Arctic of the Far North.

Most alpine tundra plants are perennials. They bloom each year from roots that have grown slowly because of long periods of dormancy. Dormancy is the plant's inactive time, when it is too cold for growth. Annual plants bloom from

seeds, but there is not adequate time on the summits for annuals to develop and produce seeds.

Many plants of the tundra have adapted to life on the exposed peaks by being "cushion" plants. They bloom in miniature swales of old and new growth that retains soil **nutrients**, moisture, and heat and serves as a sanctuary for insects just as the mountaintops serve as sanctuaries for the tundra communities.

Above *Alpine tundra, shown here in Colorado Rockies, is most distinct community of mountains.*

27

Ecologists, scientists who study the relationships of plants and animals in their environment, call these high mountain tops **refugium**, a Latin word for "refuge." During colder periods in the earth's history, Arctic plants covered far more of the mountains than they do now. When the climate warmed, forests eventually displaced tundra. The retreating tundra plants took final refuge on the mountain summits where conditions remained harsh.

The natural openings in the forests of the high Western mountains aren't as unique as the tundra gardens, but they produce the most dazzling floral displays. These openings, at various altitudes, are loosely called alpine and sub-alpine meadows. They are lusher than the low, springy alpine tundra. Growing seasons here are hurried too, and glacier fawn lilies emerge from the edges of retreating snow fields as the summer thaw begins. The bloom of alpine flowers begins at lower elevations and spreads like a rolling carpet up the slopes.

Perhaps nowhere are the vistas of wildflowers more dizzying than in the alpine meadows of Mount Rainier National Park. Each August hundreds of acres of green alpine meadows, punctuated by conifers and framed by Mount Rainier, are transformed into gardens in the clouds. While the seed stalks of early-blooming anemones blow in the wind, bear grass, paintbrush, buttercups, lupine, heath, lilies, and numerous other herbs flower in union, as if on some grand mission to color the meadows.

The Eastern mountains flame in May and June with the blooming of dogwood, redbud, and rhododendron. The mists of the Southern Appalachians turn pink when the rhododendron reach their flowering peak in late June and early July.

5 ANIMALS OF THE MOUNTAINS

Mountains are often remote and relatively free of human intrusion, factors that help make them attractive to animals. In addition, mountains often represent not only unspoiled **habitats**, but a variety of habitats, another factor attractive to many animals.

Mountain wildlife ranges from the tiny invertebrates, like the checkerspot butterflies and the **endemic** White Mountain butterfly of Mount Washington's summit, to the colorful endemic salamanders of the Smokies and the larger mountain animals of the West: bighorn sheep, mountain goats, and mountain lions.

Especially in summer, the mountains attract a crowd of animals. Various birds and mammals live throughout the mountain forests. Several species visit the high meadows and alpine country above timberline.

Opposite *Mountain lions are confined primarily to the mountains of western United States and Canada.*

The onset of winter drives most of the mountain animals to lower ground. They may leave the mountains altogether, or they may simply retire to places of food and shelter at lower, more comfortable altitudes.

Above *Pikas are among the very few animals that spend their entire life in high country, living at altitudes up to 13,500 feet.*

Not all of the mountain animals are transients. The fist-sized pika, for example, lives in the Western mountains between 8,000 and 13,500 feet. Related to rabbits, but with short, rounded ears and essentially no tail, the pika spends its entire life in the high country. It survives mountain winters by dipping into a food stash carefully prepared long before it is needed. An **herbivore**, or plant-eater, the pika begins harvesting plants in late summer. The animals let their harvest dry, then cache the dried plants in piles among the rocks for use during the winter.

Pikas avoid many of their **predators** through **camouflage**. These bright-eyed, brownish creatures are almost invisible on the rocky slopes where they live.

Marmots don't leave the high slopes either. These overstuffed ground squirrels, the Western equivalents of woodchucks, hibernate in their burrows each fall after fattening up in the wild gardens around their digs. Several kinds of small ground squirrels also live in the Western mountains.

Other common herbivores in mountain forests are mice, voles, flying squirrels—which are actually gliders rather than fliers—and various kinds of tree squirrels. Like many of the birds in mountain forests, these animals are chiefly seed, nut, and cone eaters, their

Below *The hoary marmot hibernates each winter, gobbles meadow greens in western mountains each summer.*

preference depending on the type of forest. Beavers are familiar sights along mountain streams, which they dam into ponds.

White-tail deer are common throughout most of the Eastern mountains. Several hoofed herbivores live in the Western mountains. The most enduring of them is the mountain goat, an amazingly sure-footed animal of the northwestern United States and mountainous Canada north to Alaska. The mountain goat—more accurately described as a goat-antelope—has hooves edged by thin, hard rims and cushioned by pads. The hooves provide ideal traction for navigating mountain rocks. The goat's shaggy winter coat provides warmth. When other grazing animals slip into the mountain forests and valleys, mountain goats may continue to combat winter on the upper slopes.

Another of the large mountain grazers is the bighorn sheep. Bighorns occur in several **races**, or variations, of the same basic animal. Bighorns live in many western and northwestern habitats, from desert to tundra. All of the bighorns have "footwear" adapted for climbing on rocky, mountainous slopes where they spend summers. The white Dall sheep of Canada and Alaska have

more slender horns than their southern cousins and are usually considered a distinct species.

Elk and mule deer also climb high into western mountains each summer. They tend to feed in the meadows early and late in the day and retire into the forest during the midday heat.

The offspring of mountain goats, bighorns, deer, and elk are much more likely prey for large predators than the adults. But predation, the killing of prey by predators, has little impact on their populations. Large mountain predators, like most large predators anywhere, are relatively scarce. Wolves, for instance, have just recently returned to the Rockies in Montana, having crossed the

Above *The mountain goat is perfectly adapted for life in the high western mountains. Its greatest enemy is an avalanche.*

border from Canada into Glacier National Park.

Mountain lions live primarily in the mountainous western part of Canada and the United States. Their favorite prey is deer, but they feed upon smaller animals too. A few cougars may still roam the mountain forests of the Northeast and the Southern Appalachians.

Bears are adaptable creatures, and both grizzlies and black bears were once plentiful in a wide range of habitats. Black bears are still relatively widespread throughout Canada and several states. The grizzly is rare, more or less confined to the northern Rockies and the mountains of western Canada.

Alaskan grizzlies are more numerous, and some of the biggest bruins weigh 1,700 pounds. Like their smaller cousins, the black bears, grizzlies are actually **omnivorous**, which means that they eat plant and animal material.

Smaller predators of the mountains are weasels, fishers, martens, and the Canada lynx.

Dozens of kinds of small perching birds live in mountain forests. Most birds either retreat to lower altitudes in the winter or migrate south. Some of the characteristic perching birds of Western mountains are the painted redstart, buff-

breasted flycatcher, mountain chickadee, mountain bluebird, Hammond's
flycatcher, rosy finch, green-tailed
towhee, and water pipit. The lower
Eastern mountain forests support typical
woodland species including the black-
capped chickadee, hermit thrush, black-
burnian warbler, black-throated blue
warbler, house finch, and several
woodpeckers.

Among larger perching birds, the
raven occurs in the mountains of the
West and in the Southern Appalachians.
The Steller's jay, gray-breasted jay, and
gray jay live in the Western mountains
along with the Clark's nutcracker, a
boldly marked bird that frequents
timberline.

Above *Grizzly
bears are the
largest predators in
western mountains.
Hunting and
human pressures
have nearly wiped
them out in U.S.*

Above *White-tailed ptarmigan is a year-round resident of alpine heights in West.*

The white-tailed ptarmigan is one of the exceptional animals that spends the entire year above timberline. This chicken-like bird is marvelously adapted for life on the windswept mountain crests of the West. Its legs are feathered to the toes for warmth, and it has feathered soles for snowshoes. It forages on buds, berries, and twigs, items always in supply on the tundra. Undaunted by heavy snows that cover its rations, the ptarmigan burrows under the drifts for both food and shelter.

Although a ptarmigan would prefer to run than fly, it eludes many of its predators by doing neither. The bird's drab brown feathers camouflage it on the summer tundra, and its white winter feathers hide it in the snow.

Several birds of prey live in mountainous country and several others can be seen soaring over mountains on the updrafts. Resident birds of prey in mountainous regions include peregrine falcons, great-horned owls, and great gray owls. The dominant bird of prey in the mountains is the golden eagle. A powerful bird with a six-and-one-half-foot wingspan, the golden eagle is a reasonably familiar sight in the mountainous West, but rarely seen in the East.

Less powerful but no less fascinating is the water ouzel, or American dipper. This chunky, blue-gray bird would go unnoticed were it not for its musical call and a remarkable habit: the dipper walks under water.

A resident of fast mountain streams in the West, the dipper eats water insects. Periodically it bobs to the surface, often some distance from the pool in which it disappeared. Large oil glands waterproof its feathers, membranes cover its eyes under water, and a healthy layer of fat keeps the dipper warm and dry.

Mountains are refuges for plants far from home. The high forest zone of evergreens in the Southern Appalachian Mountains has such typically Northern species as fir trees, spruce trees, and tamaracks. The mountains are also refugium for animals. The Southern Appalachians harbor Northern red-backed mice, least weasels, flying squirrels, and ravens. The relatively cold, forested bogs of the Alleghenies in the mideastern United States are a southern refuge for snowshoe hares, white-throated sparrows, golden-crowned kinglets, and other Northern animals.

6 THE FLOW OF ENERGY

In each of the mountain communities, plants and animals are engaged in an ongoing struggle for survival. In order to survive, living organisms must expend energy to function. Their energy is a product of the food they consume.

The basic food of any community is that which is produced by green plants. Through a complex process known as **photosynthesis**, green plants use sunlight in the manufacture of food. As the plant manufactures, or produces, food, it grows and eventually reproduces.

We have already read about several mountain herbivores, animals which eat plants. The herbivores are a bridge in the mountain communities between the green plants and the **carnivores**, the meat-eating hunters.

Herbivores may be tiny invertebrates, medium-sized squirrels and marmots, 300-pound bighorn rams, or a number of other animals, large and small. The common trait they share is feeding directly on plant material. By eating plants, the herbivores unlock some of the food—and energy—that has

Opposite Bighorn sheep munching on grass transfer energy from green plants to themselves.

been stored in the plant. When a predator kills and eats one of the herbivores, some of the energy originally stored by the plant, a **producer** of food, moves another link in the **food chain**.

A typical food chain in the mountains might begin with a blade of grass in an alpine meadow. A hoary marmot nibbles on the grass stem, taking nutrition from the plant. The marmot, a **consumer** of food produced by the plant, is the first link between the plant and the animals of the community in this food chain. Later, the marmot is dug from its den by a hungry grizzly bear. When the grizzly, a higher level of consumer, eats the marmot, some of the energy originally stored in the grass blade moves a second link.

None of the other large animals in the mountains will attempt to kill a grizzly. Unless a hunter kills the great bear, the bear will die eventually of natural causes. Scavengers, such as ravens, and **decomposers**, mostly microscopic bacterium and fungi, will feed upon the bear. Their efforts will eventually reduce what was once a bear to mere particles of material. In particle form, the bear will be returned to the air and soil from which, once again, green plants take some of their food and energy.

The marmot is not the only animal that eats grass, of course, and the grass, like the marmot, is involved in numerous food chains. The chains interconnect into what is called a **food web**. A food web demonstrates the diverse and complicated flow of energy within a community.

The energy flows and each species prospers as long as nothing upsets the links in the chains. In any mountain community there are several habitats, the specific places that specific animals occupy. Within each of those habitats each animal has an ecological **niche**, a job or function. The marmot habitat may be a grassy alpine meadow. Its niche as an herbivore means that it will consume plant material, perhaps whatever kind is available or perhaps just a few, favored species of plants. Its place, or role, is to keep the meadow from being overgrown by certain green plants and to provide carnivores with a source of food. Since there is a far greater mass of green plants than marmots and far more marmots than grizzly bears, each species manages to survive by using the other, but without damaging the other species as a whole.

7 CONSERVATION OF THE MOUNTAINS

The Rockies, it has often been said, are the backbone of the continent. So too, mountains are the backbone of our North American forests and much of our remaining wilderness. When we protect woodlands and unspoiled places, we are often protecting our mountains.

Fortunately, the United States and Canada have set aside millions of acres of mountain lands as national, state, and provincial parks. These are typically places of singular beauty, rich in wildlife and geologic history. One of the most remarkable preserves is the Adirondack State Park in upstate New York. Here, in one of the most populous states in America, the state has set aside 2.4 million acres of Adirondack wilderness to be "forever wild."

Beyond the preserves, many mountains have been damaged by careless development. Despite their ruggedness, mountains are slow to heal from environmental abuses. Mountain forests that are cut to the ground, for example, can easily erode. Heavy rains and melting snow, no longer absorbed by the trees, rip gullies through the slopes and carry mud into mountain streams.

Mountains also face an increasing number of environmental changes from ski resorts, residential development, gas and mineral exploration, dam building, and livestock grazing.

As they weather naturally from the effects of wind and water, mountains shrink. Because the process takes millions of years, it is not the type of thing we can readily observe. But mountain wilderness is shrinking at a rate we can observe.

We take many things from mountains—rocks, minerals, electric power, fish, game animals, and timber. We can also take delight from mountains, just the way they are.

Above *Glacier National Park in Montana Rockies is one of many mountain preserves in North America.*

GLOSSARY

alpine   a mountain location; more specifically, an area above timberline

biological   relating to a living thing

camouflage   concealment by means of blending natural coloration with the coloration of the environment

carnivore   meat-eating animal

consumer   an animal, so named because it must eat, or consume, to live

decomposer   an organism, most often bacterium and fungi, that consumes dead tissue and reduces it to small particles

dormant   a state of inactivity due to the slowing or stopping of normal functions

endemic   an organism restricted in its range to a particular, small location

food chain   the transfer of energy from green plants through a series of consuming animals

food web   the network of interlocking food chains

geologic   relating to the history of the earth and the rocks of which it is composed

glacier   a massive river of ice that forms on high ground when snowfall exceeds summer melting

habitat   an animal's or plant's immediate surrounding; its specific place within the community

herb   a flowering plant with a soft rather than woody stem

herbivore   plant-eating animal

latitude   the north or south location of a place in relation to the equator

lichen   a plant composed of both fungi and algae; a major part of Arctic vegetation

life zone   a band of distinctive plant and animal life resulting from gradual change in climate

niche   a organism's role or job in the community

nutrient   a substance providing a living organism with nourishment

omnivorous   the capability to eat both plant and animal material

photosynthesis   the process by which green plants produce simple food sugars through the use of sunlight and chlorophyll

predator   an animal that kills and feeds on other animals

producer   a green plant, so named for its ability to manufacture, or produce, food

race   variations within an animal species, usually with regard to size, color, and preferred habitat

refugium   an isolated location where displaced plants and animals survived after glaciation and climatic changes

sedge   long-stemmed, grass-like plant usually with solid triangular stems

zonation   the natural organization of plant associations in more or less parallel bands that results from variations in environmental conditions

MOUNTAIN SITES

The following is a list of sites where you can expect to find characteristic plants and animals of the mountains and outstanding mountain scenery:

CANADA

Alberta
    Banff National Park, Banff, Alberta (Canadian Rockies)
    Jasper National Park, Jasper, Alberta (Canadian Rockies)
British Columbia
    Kootenay National Park, Radium Hot Springs, British Columbia (Canadian Rockies)
    Yoho National Park, Field, British Columbia (Canadian Rockies)

UNITED STATES

Alaska
    Denali National Park, McKinley Park, Alaska (Alaska Range)
    Glacier Bay National Monument, Juneau, Alaska (St. Elias and Fairweather Mountains)
California
    Sequoia National Park, Three Rivers, California (Sierra Nevada)
    Shasta-Trinity National Forest, Redding, California (Cascade Mountains)
    Yosemite National Park, California (Sierra Nevada)
Colorado
    Rocky Mountain National Park, Estes Park, Colorado (Rocky Mountains)
    White River National Forest, Glenwood Springs, Colorado (Rocky Mountains)
Montana
    Glacier National Park, West Glacier, Montana (Rocky Mountains)
New Hampshire
    White Mountains National Forest, Laconia, New Hampshire (White Mountains)
New York
    Adirondack State Park, Albany, New York (Adirondack Mountains)
North Carolina
    Great Smoky Mountains National Park, Gatlinburg, Tennessee (Great Smoky Mountains)
    Pisgah National Forest, Asheville, North Carolina (Southern Appalachians)
Oregon
    Crater Lake National Park, Crater Lake, Oregon (Cascade Mountains)
    Mount Hood National Forest, Gresham, Oregon (Cascade Mountains)
Washington
    Mount Baker-Snoqualmie National Forest, Seattle, Washington (Cascade Mountains)
    Mount Rainier National Park, Longmire, Washington (Cascade Mountains)
    Olympic National Park, Port Angeles, Washington (Olympic Mountains)
Wyoming
    Grand Teton National Park, Moose, Wyoming (Rocky Mountains)
    Yellowstone National Park, Wyoming (Rocky Mountains)

ACTIVITIES

Here are some activities and projects that will help you learn more about the North American mountains:

1. Design a travel brochure for a particular mountain range. Describe the area's plants, animals, and scenic value. Tell what clothes would be appropriate and why. Tell how to reach the area and how someone would get around once there. Why would people want to go there? What would they be able to do there?

2. Draw a food chain or several food chains, showing the relationship of sunlight to plants, plants to animals, and animals to animals.

3. Create a collage of mountain plants and animals.

4. Build a diorama in a cardboard box. Paint a mountain background and use cardboard, clay, or plaster of Paris figures of representative mountain plants, animals, and geologic features.

INDEX

Numbers in boldface type refer to photo pages.

CONTENTS

LIST OF PARTICIPANTS

Dr. R.P. Brittain, Forensic Psychiatric Clinic, Woodside Crescent, Glasgow.

Dr. M.D. Casey, Lecturer in Human Genetics, Sheffield.

Dr. John Cowie, Consultant Psychiatrist, Putney, London.

Dr. A.W. Griffiths, Medical Officer, The Hospital, H.M. Prison, Wandsworth.

Mr. J.E. Hall Williams, Reader in Criminology in the University of London, The London School of Economics.

Dr. H. Hunter, Medical Superintendent, Balderton Hospital, Newark.

Dr. T.K. Maclachlan, Child Guidance Service, Worcester.

Dr. P.G. McGrath, Physician Superintendent, Broadmoor Hospital.

Dr. I.G.W. Pickering, Prison Department, Home Office.

Dr. E.W. Poole, E.E.G. Department, The Churchill Hospital, Oxford.

Dr. E. Slater, Department of Psychiatry, Denmark Hill, London.

Dr. D.R.K. Street, Medical Superintendent, Rampton Hospital, Retford.

Dr. T.G. Tennent, Special Hospitals Research Unit, Broadmoor Hospital.

Dr. D.J. West, Lecturer in Criminology, Institute of Criminology.

Dr. P.B. Whatmore, Consultant Psychiatrist, H.M. Prison, Perth.